The World of Human Psychology

- Ajay Kumar

Sr. No.	Name
1	Foundations of Human Psychology
2	Understanding the Brain and Behaviour
3	The Cognitive Processes
4	The Human Mind: Understanding Cognitive Processes
5	Developmental Psychology
6	Social Psychology
7	Abnormal Psychology
8	Cognitive Behavioural Therapy (CBT) and Its Applications
9	Educational Psychology: Learning and Instruction
10	The Psychology of Motivation and Achievement
11	Positive Psychology: The Science of Well-Being
12	Industrial-Organizational Psychology: Enhancing Work and Well-Being
13	Sports Psychology: Unlocking Athletic Performance
14	Forensic Psychology: Unravelling the Criminal Mind
15	Health Psychology: Promoting Wellness and Well-Being
16	Environmental Psychology: Exploring the Human-Nature Connection
17	Cross-Cultural Psychology: Understanding Human Diversity
18	Social Psychology: Exploring the Power of Social Influence
19	Personality Psychology: Unravelling the Mysteries of Individual Differences

<u>**Chapter 1: Foundations of Human Psychology**</u>

Why Study Human Psychology?

Human psychology, the scientific study of the mind and behaviour, is a discipline that has captivated the curiosity of individuals throughout history. We are all, to some extent, amateur psychologists, intrigued by the mysteries of human nature, our thoughts, emotions, and actions. But psychology, as a formal field of study, takes this innate curiosity and elevates it to a systematic and scientific level.

So, why should we study human psychology? The answer lies in its relevance to every facet of our lives. Whether we're exploring our personal relationships, delving into the intricacies of our own minds, or trying to understand the behaviour of a crowd, psychology offers invaluable insights. It provides us with tools to enhance our self-awareness, improve our interactions with others, and even make informed decisions about our careers, health, and happiness.

The applications of psychology are far-reaching. From improving mental health and well-being to enhancing workplace productivity and creating more effective educational systems, psychology plays an integral role in shaping the world around us. By understanding the fundamental principles of human psychology, we can navigate the complex terrain of human relationships, emotions, and behaviour.

Historical Overview

Psychology's roots extend deep into the history of human thought. Ancient philosophers, such as Plato and Aristotle, pondered the nature of the mind and its connection to the body. However, it was only in the late 19th century that psychology emerged as a distinct scientific discipline. Wilhelm Wundt, often referred to as the "father of psychology," established the first experimental psychology laboratory in Leipzig, Germany, in 1879.

Wundt's work marked the birth of psychology as a formal scientific endeavour. He emphasized the importance of objective observation and measurement in understanding human mental processes. As psychology evolved, different schools of thought emerged, each offering unique perspectives on human behaviour. From the psychoanalytic theories of Sigmund Freud to the behaviourism of B.F. Skinner and the humanistic psychology of Abraham Maslow, these diverse approaches have enriched our understanding of the human mind.

Major Schools of Thought

Psychology is a multifaceted discipline, and several major schools of thought have shaped its development:

1. Structuralism: Rooted in the work of Wundt, structuralism focused on breaking down mental processes into their basic components to understand the structure of consciousness.

2. Functionalism: Advocated by William James, functionalism emphasized the study of mental processes in terms of their adaptive functions, examining how they help individuals adapt to their environments.

3. Behaviourism: This school, led by John B. Watson and later B.F. Skinner, concentrated on observable behaviour and the environmental stimuli that shape it, rejecting the study of mental processes.

4. Psychoanalysis: Freud's psychoanalytic theory delved into the unconscious mind, emphasizing the role of unconscious desires and conflicts in shaping human behaviour.

5. Humanistic Psychology: Pioneered by Maslow and Carl Rogers, humanistic psychology focused on the human capacity for growth, self-actualization, and personal fulfilment.

6. Cognitive Psychology: This school, which emerged in the mid-20th century, cantered on the study of mental processes such as thinking, perception, and problem-solving.

Each of these schools of thought has contributed to the multifaceted nature of psychology. Contemporary psychology incorporates elements from various perspectives, and the field continues to evolve as new research and discoveries shed light on the complexities of human behaviour and the mind.

As we embark on this journey into the world of psychology, we will draw upon the rich history of psychological thought and delve deeper into the multifaceted dimensions of the human psyche. This exploration will provide us with a solid foundation for understanding the complexities of the human mind and behaviour that we'll encounter in the chapters to come.

Chapter 2: Understanding the Brain and Behaviour

The human brain, a three-pound mass of neural tissue encased in the skull, stands as a marvel of evolutionary design. It serves as the epicentre of human consciousness, the orchestrator of our thoughts, emotions, and behaviours. Understanding the brain's structure and function is fundamental to grasping the biological underpinnings of human behaviour.

The Structure and Function of the Brain

The brain's physical structure is divided into distinct regions, each with its own set of functions. The cerebral cortex, the outermost layer, is responsible for higher-level cognitive processes, including reasoning, problem-solving, and decision-making. Situated in the frontal lobes, this region plays a crucial role in personality and self-awareness.

Deeper within the brain lies the limbic system, often referred to as the "emotional brain." It houses structures like the amygdala and the hippocampus, which are integral to emotional regulation, memory formation, and the processing of emotional experiences. These structures work in harmony to shape our emotional responses, whether it's the rush of joy from a heartfelt moment or the gripping fear in the face of danger.

The brainstem, found at the base of the brain, controls vital functions like breathing and heartbeat. It connects the brain to the spinal cord and serves as a bridge between the body's automatic functions and higher cognitive processes.

The brain's specialization doesn't end there. The parietal lobe processes sensory information, allowing us to perceive the world around us. The occipital lobe is responsible for visual processing, the temporal lobe handles auditory perception and memory, and the motor cortex directs muscle movement. These regions collaborate seamlessly to enable us to see, hear, feel, and interact with our surroundings.

The Nervous System

The brain doesn't work in isolation; it is part of a broader communication network known as the nervous system. This intricate system consists of the central nervous system (CNS) and the peripheral nervous system (PNS).

The CNS, comprising the brain and spinal cord, serves as the command centre for processing information and making decisions. It integrates sensory data from the PNS, formulates responses, and coordinates bodily functions. The spinal cord, an extension of the brain, plays a critical role in transmitting signals to and from the brain, enabling reflex actions and motor control.

The PNS, in turn, consists of nerves and ganglia outside of the CNS. These peripheral components relay information between the CNS and the rest of the body. Sensory neurons carry data from sensory receptors to the CNS, allowing us to perceive the world. Motor neurons, on the other hand, convey commands from the CNS to muscles and glands, enabling voluntary and involuntary actions.

How Neurons Communicate

The fundamental unit of the nervous system is the neuron, a specialized cell that transmits electrical and chemical signals. Neurons communicate through a process known as neurotransmission. When a neuron receives an electrical signal, it generates a chemical signal in the form of neurotransmitters. These neurotransmitters are released into the synapse, the tiny gap between two neurons.

Upon reaching the synapse, neurotransmitters bind to receptors on the receiving neuron, initiating a new electrical signal. This process, involving the release, binding, and reuptake of neurotransmitters, enables the transmission of information from one neuron to another.

Understanding how neurons communicate is vital for comprehending the basis of our thoughts, sensations, and emotions. The balance of neurotransmitters in the brain is crucial for maintaining mental health and overall well-being. Imbalances can lead to various psychological and neurological disorders, such as depression, anxiety, and schizophrenia.

The Role of Genetics

The age-old debate of nature versus nurture continues to captivate psychologists. To what extent are our behaviours and cognitive traits determined by our genes, and how much do environmental factors contribute? Behavioural genetics, a branch of psychology, investigates these questions and reveals the complex interplay between our genetic makeup and our surroundings.

Genetics not only influence physical traits but also our predisposition to certain psychological conditions. Research involving twin and adoption studies has shed light on the heritability of various traits and disorders. These studies demonstrate that both genetic and environmental factors shape human behaviour.

The genetic basis of psychological traits remains a topic of ongoing research and debate, reflecting the intricate relationship between our genes and our experiences. As we explore the brain and behaviour further in this chapter and throughout the book, we will uncover the profound interconnections that underlie the intricacies of human thought and action.

Chapter 3: The Cognitive Processes

The human mind is a realm of boundless complexity, where thoughts, memories, and perceptions constantly interact. The study of these mental processes falls under the domain of cognitive psychology, a discipline dedicated to understanding how we perceive, think, learn, and remember. In this chapter, we embark on a journey into the inner workings of cognition, uncovering the intricacies of our mental landscape.

Perception

Perception is our window to the external world. It is the process through which we interpret sensory information from our environment, constructing a mental representation of the world around us. However, what we perceive is not a direct reflection of reality; rather, it's a subjective interpretation shaped by our sensory organs, experiences, and expectations.

Perception is a multi-step process. It begins with the reception of sensory stimuli through our senses, such as vision, hearing, taste, touch, and smell. These stimuli are then processed by our brain to create meaningful perceptual experiences. The brain employs a variety of mechanisms, including pattern recognition, depth perception, and the integration of sensory cues, to construct our perceptual reality.

Memory plays a significant role in perception. Our past experiences and stored knowledge influence how we perceive and interpret new information. This can lead to perceptual errors and biases, as well as optical illusions that challenge our understanding of reality. Understanding perception is crucial to appreciating the complexity of human cognition and how it shapes our understanding of the world.

Memory

Memory is the foundation upon which our experiences, knowledge, and identity are built. It is the cognitive process responsible for storing, retaining, and recalling information. Memory is not a monolithic construct; rather, it comprises different types and stages, each serving specific functions.

Sensory Memory: The first stage of memory, sensory memory, holds sensory information for a brief duration (usually a fraction of a second) following the initial perception. This temporary storage allows us to experience a continuous and coherent world, despite the rapid pace at which sensory input arrives.

Short-Term Memory: Short-term memory, or working memory, is the temporary holding place for information we are actively processing. It has a limited capacity and duration, typically holding around seven items for about 20-30 seconds. It is the workspace of the mind, where we manipulate and process information for problem-solving and decision-making.

Long-Term Memory: Long-term memory is the vast repository where information is stored for extended periods, ranging from minutes to a lifetime. It encompasses various types of memory, including declarative memory (explicit memory), which comprises facts and events, and procedural memory (implicit memory), which consists of skills and habits.

Memory is not a perfect system; it is subject to errors and distortions. Understanding the mechanisms of memory and factors that influence recall is essential for comprehending how our past experiences shape our present perceptions and actions.

Learning and Conditioning

Learning is the process of acquiring new knowledge, skills, or behaviours. It is a fundamental cognitive process that enables us to adapt and thrive in our ever-changing world. Learning encompasses a wide range of phenomena, from classical and operant conditioning to complex cognitive processes such as problem-solving and concept formation.

Classical Conditioning: This form of learning, famously demonstrated by Ivan Pavlov's experiments with dogs, involves the association of a neutral stimulus with an unconditioned stimulus to produce a conditioned response. Through classical conditioning, we learn to associate previously neutral stimuli with significant events, leading to the development of conditioned responses.

Operant Conditioning: B.F. Skinner introduced operant conditioning, a process that focuses on the consequences of behaviour. In operant conditioning, behaviours are reinforced or punished, leading to an increase or decrease in their frequency. This type of learning is crucial for understanding how our behaviours are shaped by the consequences they produce.

Language and Thinking

Language is a uniquely human cognitive ability, a complex system of communication that enables us to express thoughts, share information, and convey meaning. It encompasses both spoken and written forms, as well as non-verbal elements such as body language and facial expressions.

Language acquisition begins early in life, and various theories, such as Chomsky's theory of universal grammar, have been proposed to explain how humans learn language. The study of language includes syntax, semantics, pragmatics, and psycholinguistics, providing a rich terrain for cognitive exploration.

Thinking, on the other hand, is the mental process through which we manipulate and organize information to solve problems, make decisions, and generate creative ideas. Cognitive psychology delves into the intricacies of thought processes, including problem-solving strategies, decision-making biases, and the role of heuristics and cognitive biases in shaping our judgments.

In this chapter, we have scratched the surface of the cognitive processes that shape our understanding of the world and influence our behaviour.

Chapter 4: The Human Mind: Understanding Cognitive Processes

In this Chapter, we embark on a journey to explore the intricate workings of the human mind and the fascinating realm of cognitive processes. We delve into the processes that underlie how we think, reason, learn, and remember, shedding light on the cognitive machinery that makes us uniquely human.

The Cognitive Framework

Cognition is the core of human intelligence, encompassing thought, perception, memory, and problem-solving. Key concepts in this field include:

Perception: Perception is our ability to interpret sensory information and make sense of the world around us. We examine the mechanisms by which our senses create our reality.

Attention: Attention allows us to select and focus on specific information while filtering out distractions. We explore the limits and nuances of attention in our daily lives.

Memory: Memory is the repository of our experiences and knowledge. We unravel the mysteries of memory formation, storage, and retrieval, including the differences between short-term and long-term memory.

Language: Language is a unique human capacity, and we investigate its intricate structure, the psychology of language acquisition, and the cognitive processes involved in communication.

Problem-Solving and Decision-Making

Cognition involves the complex processes of problem-solving and decision-making:

Problem-Solving: Problem-solving is a cognitive endeavour that requires identifying, defining, and devising solutions for challenges. We explore the strategies and obstacles that influence our problem-solving abilities.

Decision-Making: Decision-making is a critical aspect of cognition, shaping our choices in various life situations. We examine the factors that guide our decisions, from rationality to biases and heuristics.

Theories and Models of Cognition

Cognitive psychology is rich with theories and models that attempt to explain and predict human cognition:

Information Processing Model: This model likens the mind to a computer, with information being processed through various stages like input, processing, storage, and output.

Connectionist Models: Connectionist models focus on the interconnectedness of neurons in the brain and how they process information.

Cognitive Neuroscience: Cognitive neuroscience seeks to understand cognitive processes by exploring the neural mechanisms that underlie them. We discuss how brain research contributes to our understanding of cognition.

Challenges and Ethical Considerations

Cognitive psychology faces challenges related to the ethical conduct of research, informed consent, and the potential for harm in certain experiments. Ethical considerations are paramount to ensure the well-being of research participants and the integrity of the field.

The Future of Cognitive Psychology

The future of cognitive psychology involves continued advancements in brain imaging technology, artificial intelligence, and the study of cognitive development from infancy to old age. It also encompasses the application of cognitive principles in various fields, from education to healthcare and technology.

Understanding the intricate world of cognitive processes empowers us to appreciate the complexities of the human mind. It provides insights into how we perceive, learn, and make decisions, shedding light on the core of human intelligence and paving the way for future discoveries and applications in the field of cognitive psychology.

Chapter 5: Developmental Psychology

Human life is a journey of growth and transformation, marked by continuous change and development from infancy to old age. Developmental psychology is the study of these remarkable transformations, exploring the physical, cognitive, social, and emotional changes that occur at different stages of life. In this chapter, we embark on a voyage through the various life stages, uncovering the complex processes that shape human development.

Lifespan Development

Lifespan development, a core concept in developmental psychology, emphasizes that human growth and change occur throughout the entirety of life. From the moment of conception to the final breath, individuals undergo a series of developmental stages, each marked by distinct challenges, milestones, and transitions. This perspective acknowledges that development is a lifelong process, influenced by a dynamic interplay of genetic, environmental, and cultural factors.

Prenatal Development: The journey of human development begins before birth, in the prenatal stage. Here, the miracle of life unfolds as a single fertilized cell evolves into a complex organism with an intricate network of organs and systems. Prenatal development is divided into three main stages: the germinal stage, the embryonic stage, and the fatal stage. It is a period of astonishing transformation, where genetic inheritance meets environmental influences.

Infancy and Early Childhood: The first years of life are marked by rapid physical and sensory-motor development. Infants learn to navigate their surroundings, develop attachment bonds with caregivers, and explore the world through their senses. The roots of language and social understanding are established during this period, laying the foundation for later development.

Adolescence: Adolescence is a stage characterized by physical maturation, cognitive growth, and the quest for identity. This is a time of exploration and self-discovery, as individuals grapple with issues of autonomy, peer relationships, and identity formation. The brain undergoes significant changes during this period, impacting decision-making and emotional regulation.

Adulthood: Adulthood encompasses a wide range of experiences, from early adulthood to middle age and beyond. It is marked by shifts in family and work roles, as well as the pursuit of personal and professional goals. Cognitive development continues, and social relationships become increasingly complex.

Aging and Old Age: The final stage of the human lifespan is old age, a time of reflection and adaptation. While physical decline is a part of the aging process, it is also a period of potential wisdom and contentment. Individuals face unique challenges related to health, relationships, and meaning in life.

Theories of Development

Developmental psychology is guided by various theoretical perspectives that help explain the processes and influences behind human growth. Several notable theories have shaped our understanding of human development:

Psychoanalytic Theories: Sigmund Freud's psychoanalytic theory introduced the idea of unconscious conflicts shaping behaviour. Erik Erikson's psychosocial theory expanded on Freud's work, emphasizing the importance of social and emotional development throughout the lifespan.

Cognitive Theories: Cognitive theories, such as Jean Piaget's cognitive development theory, emphasize the role of cognitive processes, like schema formation and adaptation, in shaping human development.

Social and Environmental Theories: Social learning theories, like Albert Bandura's social cognitive theory, underscore the impact of social modelling and reinforcement in development. Environmental theories, such as Uriel Bronfenbrenner's ecological systems theory, highlight the influence of the environment, culture, and society on development.

Key Stages: Childhood, Adolescence, Adulthood, and Aging

Each stage of life brings its unique set of developmental tasks and challenges. Childhood is marked by the acquisition of language, the development of attachment, and the growth of cognitive skills. Adolescence is a time of identity exploration and peer relationships. Adulthood involves building relationships, pursuing careers, and establishing a sense of purpose. Aging is a period of reflection, adaptation, and the pursuit of meaningful experiences.

Understanding these stages and the associated developmental changes is vital for parents, educators, psychologists, and anyone interested in comprehending the complex process of human development. It sheds light on the profound transformations that shape our lives and influence our understanding of ourselves and those around us.

Chapter 6: Social Psychology

The human experience is inherently social. From our interactions with friends and family to our connections with strangers, social psychology delves into the intricate web of human relationships, investigating how we perceive, influence, and interact with others. In this chapter, we explore the fascinating realm of social psychology and the myriad factors that shape our social behaviours and attitudes.

Social Influence

One of the fundamental areas of study in social psychology is social influence. This concept examines the ways in which individuals are affected by the presence, actions, and opinions of others. Social influence manifests in various forms, including conformity, compliance, and obedience.

Conformity: Conformity is the tendency to adjust one's thoughts, feelings, or behaviours to align with the attitudes and behaviours of a group or the prevailing social norms. Experiments like Solomon Asch's conformity studies have revealed the power of social pressure in influencing our choices and decisions.

Compliance: Compliance is the act of agreeing to a request or suggestion from another person. Techniques like the foot-in-the-door, door-in-the-face, and the mere presence of others can influence individuals to comply with requests, whether they align with their preferences or not.

Obedience: Obedience involves following the commands of an authority figure. Stanley Milgram's famous obedience experiments demonstrated the extent to which individuals might follow instructions, even if they contradict their moral beliefs. These studies highlighted the powerful influence of authority figures in shaping human behaviour.

Group Dynamics

The study of social psychology also encompasses the complexities of group dynamics, exploring how individuals behave when part of a group. Several key concepts underpin this area of research:

Groupthink: Groupthink is a phenomenon where group members prioritize group cohesion and consensus over critical thinking and problem-solving. It can lead to poor decision-making and reluctance to challenge group norms.

Social Loafing: Social loafing occurs when individuals exert less effort when working in a group compared to when working alone. This phenomenon highlights the balance between individual and collective responsibility in group settings.

Deindividuation: Deindividuation occurs when individuals lose self-awareness and self-restraint in group situations, leading to behaviours they might not engage in otherwise. This concept helps explain instances of mob behaviour and the influence of crowds.

Social Identity: Social identity theory explores how individuals categorize themselves and others into various social groups, influencing their social attitudes and behaviours. Our social identities can lead to in-group favouritism and out-group discrimination.

Prejudice and Discrimination

Prejudice and discrimination are pervasive issues in social psychology, delving into the negative attitudes and behaviours directed toward individuals or groups based on their characteristics, such as race, gender, religion, or social class.

Implicit Bias: Implicit bias refers to unconscious and automatic attitudes and stereotypes that influence our judgments and behaviour. Understanding implicit bias is critical in addressing and combating prejudiced attitudes.

Stereotypes: Stereotypes are generalized beliefs about the characteristics and attributes of particular social groups. They can lead to biases and discriminatory actions when individuals are judged based on these generalizations.

In-Group and Out-Group Dynamics: In-group bias refers to the preference for one's own social group, while out-group derogation is the tendency to view members of other groups more negatively. These dynamics contribute to the formation of stereotypes and the perpetuation of prejudice.

Attraction and Relationships

Social psychology also explores the dynamics of attraction, love, and relationships. Theories like the social exchange theory and the triangular theory of love provide insight into the factors that influence our romantic and interpersonal relationships. Additionally, concepts like interpersonal attraction and the mere exposure effect shed light on the mechanisms that underlie our social connections.

Aggression and Altruism

The study of social behaviour extends to aggression and altruism, examining the causes and consequences of violent behaviour as well as the motivations behind helping and prosocial actions. Understanding the roots of aggression and the factors that promote altruism is essential for promoting social harmony and reducing conflict.

In this chapter, we have touched on some of the key topics within social psychology, revealing the complex interplay of social influence, group dynamics, prejudice, attraction, and behaviour.

Chapter 7: Abnormal Psychology

Human behaviour is incredibly diverse, and what is considered normal or abnormal varies across cultures and contexts. Abnormal psychology is the field that seeks to understand, classify, and treat psychological disorders—conditions that deviate from what is considered typical or healthy. In this chapter, we delve into the intricate world of abnormal psychology, examining the various psychological disorders, their causes, and the approaches to treatment.

Psychological Disorders

Psychological disorders, often referred to as mental disorders, encompass a wide range of conditions that affect an individual's thoughts, emotions, behaviours, and overall well-being. These disorders can be temporary or chronic, mild or severe, and may manifest in various ways. Common psychological disorders include:

Mood Disorders: Mood disorders, such as depression and bipolar disorder, involve disturbances in a person's mood, leading to feelings of sadness, hopelessness, or extreme mood swings.

Anxiety Disorders: Anxiety disorders, like generalized anxiety disorder, panic disorder, and social anxiety disorder, are characterized by excessive worry, fear, or anxiety that can interfere with daily life.

Schizophrenia and Other Psychotic Disorders: Schizophrenia is a severe disorder marked by distorted thinking, delusions, hallucinations, and disorganized behaviour. Other psychotic disorders share some of these features.

Personality Disorders: Personality disorders, including borderline, narcissistic, and antisocial personality disorders, involve enduring patterns of behaviour, cognition, and inner experience that deviate from cultural expectations.

Eating Disorders: Eating disorders, such as anorexia nervosa and bulimia nervosa, involve severe disturbances in eating behaviour and body image.

Substance-Related and Addictive Disorders: Substance-related disorders pertain to problematic use of alcohol, drugs, or other substances, leading to physical, psychological, or social harm. Behavioural addictions, such as gambling addiction, fall into this category.

Neurodevelopmental Disorders: Conditions like autism spectrum disorder and attention-deficit/hyperactivity disorder (ADHD) emerge in childhood and involve difficulties in social interactions, communication, or cognitive functioning.

Mental Health Disorders in Childhood and Adolescence: Conditions that primarily affect children and adolescents, including oppositional defiant disorder and conduct disorder, are of particular concern.

Causes of Psychological Disorders

The ethology of psychological disorders is multifaceted and can involve a complex interplay of genetic, biological, psychological, and environmental factors. While the specific causes vary from one disorder to another, some common factors include:

Biological Factors: Genetics, brain chemistry, and neurological functioning can play a role in the development of certain disorders. For example, schizophrenia is believed to have a genetic component.

Psychological Factors: Early life experiences, trauma, and coping mechanisms can contribute to the development of disorders like post-traumatic stress disorder (PTSD) and dissociative disorders.

Environmental Factors: Adverse life events, such as childhood abuse or neglect, can increase the risk of developing disorders like depression and anxiety.

Social and Cultural Factors: Cultural norms and societal expectations can influence the expression of certain disorders, as well as the stigma attached to seeking help.

Diagnosis and Assessment

The diagnosis of psychological disorders is a complex process that involves the assessment of symptoms, behaviours, and the individual's personal history. The Diagnostic and Statistical Manual of Mental Disorders (DSM-5) is a widely used resource that provides a framework for classifying and diagnosing psychological disorders. Assessment methods can include clinical interviews, psychological testing, and observation.

Treatment Approaches

Psychological disorders are often treatable, and various approaches are available to help individuals manage their symptoms and improve their quality of life.

Treatment methods can include:

Psychotherapy: Psychotherapy, or talk therapy, is a common treatment approach that involves working with a trained therapist to explore thoughts, feelings, and behaviours. Various forms of psychotherapy, including cognitive-behavioural therapy (CBT), psychoanalytic therapy, and dialectical-behaviour therapy (DBT), are employed to address different types of disorders.

Medication: Medications are frequently used in the treatment of disorders like depression, anxiety, and schizophrenia. These medications can help manage symptoms and improve an individual's overall well-being.

Hospitalization and Inpatient Treatment: In severe cases or during a crisis, individuals may require hospitalization or inpatient treatment to provide a safe and structured environment for stabilization and treatment.

Supportive Services: Community-based support services and self-help groups can also be invaluable in helping individuals manage their conditions and maintain a fulfilling life.

Stigma and Advocacy

Stigma surrounding mental health issues remains a significant barrier to seeking help and receiving treatment. Reducing this stigma and advocating for better mental health resources and support is crucial in addressing the challenges faced by individuals with psychological disorders.

Chapter 8: Cognitive Behavioural Therapy (CBT) and Its Applications

Cognitive Behavioural Therapy, often abbreviated as CBT, is a prominent and versatile approach within the field of psychology. It has proven effective in treating a wide range of psychological issues, making it one of the most widely practiced forms of psychotherapy. This chapter delves into the foundations of CBT, its principles, and applications in various contexts.

Understanding CBT

Cognitive Behavioural Therapy is rooted in the belief that our thoughts, feelings, and behaviours are interconnected, and altering negative thought patterns can lead to positive changes in feelings and actions. The foundational principles of CBT can be summarized as follows:

Cognitive Restructuring: CBT recognizes that negative or irrational thought patterns can contribute to emotional distress and maladaptive behaviours. The process of cognitive restructuring involves identifying these distorted thoughts, challenging them, and replacing them with more rational, balanced, and positive thoughts.

Behavioural Techniques: CBT emphasizes the importance of changing behaviour as a means of improving mental health. This may involve setting goals, learning problem-solving skills, and engaging in exposure therapy to confront and overcome fears and anxieties.

Collaborative and Time-Limited: CBT is typically a short-term, focused therapy that involves active collaboration between the therapist and the individual. The therapist helps the individual identify and address specific issues, providing practical strategies for managing them.

Empirical Support: CBT is considered evidence-based because it has garnered extensive empirical support through research and clinical trials. Its effectiveness in treating a wide array of conditions, including depression, anxiety disorders, and post-traumatic stress disorder (PTSD), is well-documented.

Applications of CBT

CBT can be applied to various psychological issues and in different settings. Some of its notable applications include:

Depression: CBT has been particularly effective in treating depression. It helps individuals recognize and challenge their negative thought patterns and develop healthier perspectives on themselves and their situations.

Anxiety Disorders: CBT is a preferred treatment for various anxiety disorders, such as generalized anxiety disorder, social anxiety disorder, and specific phobias. Exposure therapy, a component of CBT, is often used to gradually desensitize individuals to their fears.

Post-Traumatic Stress Disorder (PTSD): CBT, particularly cognitive processing therapy (CPT) and prolonged exposure therapy (PE), has been successful in helping individuals with PTSD process traumatic events and manage their symptoms.

Obsessive-Compulsive Disorder (OCD): Exposure and response prevention (ERP), a specialized form of CBT, is a leading treatment for OCD. It involves gradually exposing individuals to their obsessive thoughts and preventing the associated compulsive behaviours.

Substance Use Disorders: CBT is used to help individuals struggling with substance abuse by addressing the cognitive and behavioural aspects of addiction. It teaches coping skills and strategies to prevent relapse.

Eating Disorders: CBT is employed in the treatment of eating disorders like bulimia and binge-eating disorder. It helps individuals challenge their distorted body image and eating-related thoughts.

Chronic Pain Management: CBT can assist individuals in managing chronic pain by changing their responses to pain and improving their coping strategies.

Insomnia: Cognitive Behavioural Therapy for Insomnia (CBT-I) is a well-established treatment for sleep disorders. It focuses on changing thoughts and behaviours related to sleep, promoting healthier sleep patterns.

Online and Self-Help Applications

In recent years, CBT has been adapted for online and self-help applications. Internet-based CBT programs, guided by qualified therapists or as self-directed resources, provide accessibility to therapy for those who may face barriers to in-person treatment.

Challenges and Future Directions

While CBT has proven highly effective, it is not without challenges. Some individuals may not respond to CBT, and access to qualified CBT therapists can be limited in certain regions. The future of CBT lies in continued research to refine and adapt its techniques, making them even more accessible and effective.

Educational psychology is the branch of psychology that focuses on understanding how people learn and how teaching and instructional methods can facilitate effective learning. In this chapter, we explore the key principles of educational psychology, including the science of learning, cognitive development, and effective teaching strategies.

The Science of Learning

Learning is a fundamental aspect of human development, and educational psychology seeks to unravel the processes that underlie it. Several key concepts in the science of learning include:

Cognitive Processes: Learning is a cognitive process that involves acquiring knowledge, understanding concepts, and developing problem-solving skills. It encompasses various mental activities, such as attention, memory, and reasoning.

Memory: Memory is a critical component of learning. It involves the encoding, storage, and retrieval of information. Researchers have identified various memory systems, including sensory memory, short-term memory, and long-term memory, each playing a role in the learning process.

Motivation: Motivation is a central factor in learning. Individuals are more likely to learn and excel when they are motivated. Educational psychologists study the sources of motivation and how to foster it in educational settings.

Metacognition: Metacognition refers to the awareness and regulation of one's own thinking and learning processes. It involves planning, monitoring, and evaluating one's learning strategies.

Cognitive Development and Learning Theories

Educational psychologists draw from various learning theories to understand how individuals acquire knowledge and skills:

Piaget's Theory of Cognitive Development: Jean Piaget's theory posits that cognitive development unfolds in distinct stages, each characterized by particular cognitive abilities. This theory emphasizes the importance of adapting instruction to a child's developmental stage.

Vygotsky's Socio-Cultural Theory: Lev Vygotsky's theory highlights the role of social interactions and cultural context in learning. He introduced the concept of the zone of proximal development (ZPD), which represents the tasks that learners can accomplish with the support of a more knowledgeable individual.

Information Processing Theory: This theory likens the human mind to a computer, emphasizing the role of attention, memory, and problem-solving in learning.

Behaviourism and Conditioning: Behaviourist theories, like classical and operant conditioning, emphasize the role of reinforcement and conditioning in learning. These theories are particularly relevant in understanding how behaviours are shaped and maintained in educational settings.

Effective Teaching Strategies

Educational psychology provides valuable insights into effective teaching methods. Some of these strategies include:

Active Learning: Active learning methods encourage students to engage with the material through discussion, problem-solving, and hands-on activities. These methods promote deeper understanding and retention of information.

Individualized Instruction: Tailoring instruction to the individual needs and learning styles of students can enhance the learning experience. This may involve differentiating instruction, using personalized learning plans, or providing accommodations for students with diverse needs.

Feedback and Assessment: Providing timely and constructive feedback to students is essential for their growth. Formative assessment, where teachers gather ongoing information about student progress, is a valuable tool for improving learning outcomes.

Technology in Education: The integration of technology in education, such as online learning platforms, educational software, and multimedia resources, offers new avenues for instruction and assessment.

Collaborative Learning: Encouraging collaboration and group work in the classroom fosters social interactions and shared knowledge, which can enhance learning.

The Challenges of Educational Psychology

Educational psychology faces challenges such as educational disparities, the digital divide, and the need for culturally responsive teaching methods. Researchers in this field continue to explore innovative solutions to address these challenges and promote equitable education for all.

In the subsequent chapters, we will explore specific applications of educational psychology, such as the psychology of motivation, the role of technology in education, and strategies for effective teaching and assessment. These insights will help educators and learners better understand the processes of learning and the most effective ways to facilitate it.

Chapter 10: The Psychology of Motivation and Achievement

Motivation is the driving force that underlies our thoughts, behaviours, and actions. It plays a central role in our pursuit of goals, our willingness to exert effort, and our determination to overcome challenges. In this chapter, we delve into the psychology of motivation and achievement, exploring the factors that inspire us to reach our full potential.

Understanding Motivation

Motivation is a multifaceted concept that encompasses a range of internal and external factors, both conscious and unconscious, that energize and direct our behaviour. Key aspects of motivation include:

Intrinsic and Extrinsic Motivation: Intrinsic motivation arises from within, driven by personal interest or the satisfaction of the activity itself. Extrinsic motivation, on the other hand, is fuelled by external factors such as rewards or recognition.

Self-Determination Theory: Self-determination theory posits that individuals are most motivated when they feel a sense of autonomy, competence, and relatedness in their pursuits.

Goal Setting: Goals serve as powerful motivators. Setting specific, achievable, and challenging goals can drive individuals to accomplish tasks and pursue their aspirations.

Expectancy Theory: Expectancy theory suggests that motivation is influenced by an individual's belief in their ability to achieve a goal and the expectation of receiving a reward or outcome.

Types of Motivation

Motivation can take on different forms, including:

Achievement Motivation: Achievement motivation is the drive to excel, to reach one's potential, and to set high standards for oneself. It often leads to the pursuit of challenging goals and a commitment to personal growth.

Social Motivation: Social motivation is the desire to connect with others, form relationships, and gain social acceptance. It plays a significant role in our interactions with friends, family, and society as a whole.

Mastery Motivation: Mastery motivation involves the pursuit of skills and knowledge for their intrinsic value. It is associated with a love of learning and the joy of mastering new abilities.

Fear of Failure and Fear of Success: Fear of failure can be a powerful motivator, driving individuals to avoid making mistakes. Fear of success, on the other hand, can create anxiety about the responsibilities and expectations that come with achieving one's goals.

Factors Influencing Motivation

Several factors can influence an individual's motivation, including:

Self-Efficacy: Self-efficacy, a concept introduced by Albert Bandura, refers to an individual's belief in their ability to perform a specific task or achieve a particular goal. High self-efficacy is associated with increased motivation and perseverance.

Attribution Theory: Attribution theory explores how individuals explain their successes and failures. Attribution style can impact motivation, with individuals who attribute success to their efforts being more motivated to pursue challenging goals.

External Rewards and Incentives: External rewards, such as money or recognition, can provide motivation, but they may not always lead to sustained interest in a task. In some cases, overreliance on external rewards can undermine intrinsic motivation.

Procrastination: Procrastination is a common challenge in motivation. Understanding the underlying reasons for procrastination, such as fear of failure or task aversion, can help individuals address and overcome this obstacle.

Achievement and Success

Achievement and success are closely tied to motivation. Successful individuals often share common traits, such as perseverance, resilience, and a strong work ethic. However, success is a multifaceted concept that extends beyond material accomplishments to include personal growth, fulfilment, and a sense of purpose.

The Role of Motivation in Education and Career

Motivation plays a pivotal role in both education and career pursuits. In education, motivating students is essential for promoting engagement and academic achievement. In the workplace, motivation influences job performance, career advancement, and job satisfaction.

Achieving Balance and Well-Being

Balancing motivation with self-care and well-being is crucial. Overemphasis on achievement and success can lead to burnout and negatively impact mental and physical health. Finding a harmonious balance between ambition and well-being is an essential aspect of a fulfilling life.

In the subsequent chapters, we will explore motivation within various contexts, including education, work, and personal development.

Understanding the science of motivation can empower individuals to set and achieve their goals while maintaining a healthy and balanced life.

Chapter 11: Positive Psychology: The Science of Well-Being

Positive psychology is a branch of psychology that focuses on the study of human strengths, well-being, and the factors that contribute to a fulfilling and flourishing life. In this chapter, we delve into the principles of positive psychology and the pathways to happiness and well-being.

The Birth of Positive Psychology

Positive psychology emerged in the late 20th century as a response to the traditional focus on pathology and mental illness within psychology. Martin Seligman, often considered the founding figure of positive psychology, sought to redirect the field's attention toward the study of happiness, strengths, and positive human experiences.

Key Concepts in Positive Psychology

Positive psychology encompasses several key concepts and principles, including:

Subjective Well-Being: Subjective well-being is a central concept in positive psychology. It involves the individual's personal evaluation of their life and overall sense of happiness and satisfaction. Components of subjective well-being include life satisfaction, positive emotions, and a sense of purpose.

Character Strengths and Virtues: Positive psychology explores character strengths that enable individuals to live a good life and contribute to the well-being of others. The Values in Action (VIA) classification identifies 24 character strengths, including kindness, gratitude, and perseverance.

Flow: Flow is a state of optimal experience where individuals are fully immersed in an activity, experiencing deep concentration and enjoyment. Achieving flow often leads to heightened well-being.

Positive Emotions: Positive psychology emphasizes the importance of cultivating positive emotions like gratitude, joy, and love. These emotions can enhance well-being and contribute to resilience in the face of challenges.

Paths to Well-Being

Positive psychology offers several paths to well-being and fulfilment:

Gratitude: Practicing gratitude by acknowledging and appreciating the positive aspects of life can increase happiness and life satisfaction.

Mindfulness: Mindfulness involves paying attention to the present moment without judgment. Mindfulness practices, such as meditation, can reduce stress and enhance well-being.

Savouring: Savouring is the act of fully enjoying and appreciating positive experiences. It involves taking the time to relish moments of joy and happiness.

Positive Relationships: Positive psychology highlights the importance of positive relationships and social connections in promoting well-being. Building and maintaining strong relationships can enhance life satisfaction.

Resilience: Resilience is the ability to bounce back from adversity and challenges. Positive psychology focuses on developing resilience as a key factor in well-being.

Applications of Positive Psychology

Positive psychology has practical applications in various fields, including:

Therapy and Counselling: Positive psychology interventions can be incorporated into therapy to help individuals overcome depression, anxiety, and other mental health challenges.

Education: Positive psychology principles can be used in educational settings to promote a positive classroom environment, enhance student engagement, and foster character development.

Workplace: In the workplace, positive psychology interventions can improve employee well-being, job satisfaction, and productivity.

Health and Wellness: Positive psychology interventions can contribute to overall health and well-being by reducing stress and promoting healthy behaviours.

Challenges and Criticisms

While positive psychology offers valuable insights into well-being, it is not without challenges. Critics argue that focusing solely on positive aspects of life may neglect the importance of addressing and understanding negative experiences and emotions. A balanced approach is essential for a comprehensive understanding of human well-being.

The Pursuit of a Fulfilling Life

Positive psychology invites individuals to actively engage in the pursuit of a fulfilling and meaningful life. By cultivating strengths, fostering positive emotions, and building resilience, individuals can enhance their well-being and lead a life characterized by happiness, purpose, and flourishing.

In the following chapters, we will explore specific applications of positive psychology, including its role in mental health, Industrial-Organization psychology and work, and personal development. Understanding the principles of positive psychology can empower individuals to lead more fulfilling and contented lives.

Chapter 12: Industrial-Organizational Psychology: Enhancing Work and Well-Being

Industrial-Organizational (I-O) psychology is a field that applies psychological principles to the workplace, aiming to improve the well-being of employees, the effectiveness of organizations, and the overall functioning of the workplace. In this chapter, we explore the core concepts of I-O psychology and its impact on the world of work.

Understanding Industrial-Organizational Psychology

I-O psychology encompasses various aspects related to work and organizations, including:

Personnel Psychology: Personnel psychology focuses on the selection, assessment, training, and development of employees. It aims to match individuals with the right job roles and enhance their performance.

Organizational Psychology: Organizational psychology delves into the dynamics of organizations, examining issues like leadership, motivation, culture, and change management. It seeks to optimize the functioning of organizations and the well-being of employees.

Work-Life Balance: I-O psychology addresses the balance between work and personal life, emphasizing the importance of employee well-being and job satisfaction.

Occupational Health Psychology: Occupational health psychology concentrates on promoting health and safety in the workplace, as well as addressing issues like stress and burnout.

Selection and Assessment

I-O psychologists play a crucial role in employee selection and assessment. They develop and validate selection tests, interview protocols, and assessment tools to identify the right candidates for specific job roles. This process ensures a good fit between individuals and their job responsibilities.

Training and Development

I-O psychologists design training programs to enhance employee skills and knowledge. They consider factors like adult learning principles and the transfer of training to ensure that employees can effectively apply what they have learned in their jobs.

Leadership and Management

I-O psychology addresses leadership and management within organizations. It explores effective leadership styles, the development of leadership competencies, and methods for improving employee morale and engagement.

Workplace Culture and Climate

Organizational culture and climate are essential in promoting well-being and productivity. I-O psychologists assess, analyse, and help shape these aspects to create a positive work environment.

Workplace Motivation

Motivation is a key factor in employee performance. I-O psychologists study motivational factors and design interventions to boost motivation, such as rewards and recognition programs.

Stress and Well-Being

Occupational health psychology addresses stress, burnout, and mental health issues in the workplace. I-O psychologists work to reduce stressors, enhance well-being, and provide support for employees facing mental health challenges.

Challenges and Ethical Considerations

I-O psychology is not without challenges and ethical considerations. Some of these challenges include addressing workplace diversity, managing conflicts of interest, and balancing the needs of employees and organizations. Ethical considerations are vital in maintaining the integrity and credibility of the field.

The Future of I-O Psychology

The future of I-O psychology includes addressing evolving workplace dynamics, such as remote work and the gig economy. Additionally, the field will continue to emphasize employee well-being and mental health.

I-O psychology plays a crucial role in fostering positive work environments, enhancing employee well-being, and contributing to the effectiveness and success of organizations. Understanding its principles and practices can help individuals, organizations, and society as a whole create more satisfying and productive workplaces.

Chapter 13: Sports Psychology: Unlocking Athletic Performance

Sports psychology is a specialized field that explores the psychological factors that impact athletic performance and participation in sports. In this chapter, we delve into the principles of sports psychology, from enhancing motivation to managing pressure, and how it plays a pivotal role in the world of sports.

The Psychology of Athletic Performance

Sports psychology encompasses several key areas that contribute to athletic performance:

Motivation: Motivation is a driving force in sports. Sports psychologists work with athletes to enhance their intrinsic motivation and focus on their goals, helping them persist through rigorous training and competitions.

Mental Toughness: Mental toughness involves resilience, self-discipline, and the ability to withstand pressure and adversity. Athletes strive to develop mental resilience to perform at their best.

Concentration and Focus: Maintaining focus amid distractions is crucial in sports. Techniques such as visualization and mindfulness help athletes stay concentrated during competition.

Self-Confidence: Self-confidence is vital for athletes. Sports psychologists work on building and maintaining athletes' self-belief, enabling them to face challenges with a positive mind-set.

Stress and Anxiety Management: The pressure of competition can lead to stress and anxiety. Sports psychology techniques, like relaxation exercises and cognitive restructuring, help athletes manage these emotions.

Performance Enhancement Strategies

Sports psychologists employ various strategies to enhance athletic performance:

Imagery and Visualization: Visualization involves mentally rehearsing movements and scenarios, which can improve motor skills and reduce anxiety. Athletes visualize successful performances to boost confidence.

Goal Setting: Goal setting involves establishing specific, measurable, and time-bound objectives. Athletes use this technique to provide direction and motivation for their training and performance.

Pre-Competition Routines: Developing pre-competition routines helps athletes prepare mentally and physically before an event. These routines can instil confidence and readiness.

Biofeedback and Relaxation Techniques: Biofeedback involves monitoring physiological responses, such as heart rate and muscle tension, to promote relaxation and self-regulation.

Cognitive Behavioural Techniques: Cognitive behavioural therapy (CBT) helps athletes recognize and change irrational beliefs and negative thought patterns that hinder performance.

The Role of Sports Psychology in Different Sports

Sports psychology is applicable to various sports, from individual endeavours like tennis and golf to team sports such as soccer and basketball. Each sport has its unique psychological demands, and sports psychologists tailor their approaches to suit the specific needs of athletes.

Challenges and Ethical Considerations

Sports psychology faces challenges, including the stigma associated with seeking psychological help in sports and the ethical dilemmas related to the use of performance-enhancing substances. Ethical practice and confidentiality are paramount in maintaining the integrity of sports psychology.

The Future of Sports Psychology

The future of sports psychology involves continued research into mental training techniques, the integration of technology for monitoring performance and psychological states, and addressing mental health issues in athletes.

Sports psychology is a dynamic field that empowers athletes to unlock their full potential, manage stress, and achieve peak performance. Understanding the principles of sports psychology can benefit athletes, coaches, and individuals in various sports-related roles, contributing to the overall advancement of athletic achievement and well-being.

Chapter 14: Forensic Psychology: Unravelling the Criminal Mind

Forensic psychology is a field that applies psychological principles to the legal and criminal justice systems. It involves understanding and addressing various aspects of criminal behaviour, legal processes, and the intersection of psychology and the law. In this chapter, we explore the core concepts of forensic psychology and its role in the criminal justice system.

The Intersection of Psychology and Law

Forensic psychology encompasses a wide range of topics and activities, including:

Criminal Profiling: Criminal profiling involves creating profiles of potential suspects based on behaviour patterns, psychological characteristics, and other evidence. Profilers aim to assist law enforcement in solving crimes and identifying offenders.

Witness Memory and Testimony: Forensic psychologists examine the reliability of witness memory and testimony in legal proceedings. They may assess factors that affect eyewitness identification and recall.

Competency and Insanity Evaluations: Forensic psychologists evaluate individuals' mental competency to stand trial and their sanity at the time of an alleged crime. These evaluations help determine if individuals are fit for legal proceedings and can be held criminally responsible for their actions.

Criminal Behaviour and Risk Assessment: Forensic psychologists study criminal behaviour patterns, risk factors, and recidivism. They help assess and manage the risk posed by individuals involved in the criminal justice system.

Victimology: Victimology explores the psychological impact of crime on victims. It examines the emotional, physical, and social consequences of victimization.

Psychological Evaluations and Assessments

Forensic psychologists conduct psychological evaluations and assessments in various legal contexts:

Criminal Sentencing: They may provide assessments that help judges and legal professionals determine appropriate sentences, treatment options, or parole decisions.

Child Custody and Family Law: In family court, forensic psychologists evaluate issues related to child custody, visitation, and parenting plans, with the goal of ensuring the best interests of the child.

Civil Commitment: Forensic psychologists assess individuals who are considered a danger to themselves or others and may require involuntary psychiatric treatment or commitment.

Risk Assessment and Parole: In correctional settings, they assess the risk of reoffending and provide recommendations for parole or release decisions.

Witness Competency: Forensic psychologists assess the competency of witnesses, helping determine if they are capable of providing reliable testimony in legal proceedings.

Challenges and Ethical Considerations

Forensic psychology faces ethical considerations, such as ensuring impartiality, avoiding conflicts of interest, and maintaining confidentiality within the bounds of the law. Ethical practice is essential in upholding the integrity of the field and preserving the rights of individuals involved in legal cases.

The Future of Forensic Psychology

The future of forensic psychology involves advancements in the assessment of risk, treatment of offenders, and the integration of psychological insights into legal proceedings. Additionally, the field will continue to address the ethical challenges that arise in the intersection of psychology and the law.

Forensic psychology plays a pivotal role in the criminal justice system, helping to understand criminal behaviour, assess individuals' mental states, and ensure that legal processes are conducted fairly and in compliance with psychological principles. Understanding the principles and practices of forensic psychology can provide valuable insights into the workings of the legal system and its interface with the human mind.

Chapter 15: Health Psychology: Promoting Wellness and Well-Being

Health psychology is a field that explores the interplay between psychological factors and physical health. It focuses on understanding how thoughts, emotions, behaviours, and social factors influence health and well-being. In this chapter, we delve into the principles of health psychology and its role in promoting a healthy and fulfilling life.

The Mind-Body Connection

Health psychology acknowledges the intricate relationship between the mind and the body. Key concepts in this field include:

Psychosomatic Illness: Psychosomatic illness refers to physical conditions that are influenced by psychological factors. Stress, for example, can exacerbate conditions like asthma, irritable bowel syndrome, and migraines.

Placebo Effect: The placebo effect is the phenomenon where an individual experiences improvements in health or symptoms solely due to their belief in a treatment's effectiveness, even if the treatment lacks active ingredients.

Stress and Health: Stress is a central focus in health psychology. Chronic stress can lead to a range of health problems, including cardiovascular issues, immune system suppression, and mental health challenges.

Positive Psychology and Health: Positive psychology principles are applied to health psychology, emphasizing strengths, resilience, and well-being as factors that promote health and recovery.

Promoting Health and Well-Being

Health psychology employs various strategies to promote wellness and well-being:

Health Behaviour Change: Health psychologists work with individuals to modify behaviours that impact health, such as smoking, unhealthy eating, and physical inactivity. They help individuals set and achieve health-related goals.

Preventive Medicine: Health psychology plays a role in preventive medicine, encouraging regular check-ups, vaccinations, and screenings to detect health issues before they become serious.

Adherence to Medical Treatment: Ensuring that patients adhere to prescribed medical treatments and follow-up care is a crucial aspect of health psychology. Adherence can lead to better health outcomes.

Coping with Illness: Health psychologist's help individuals cope with chronic illnesses, manage pain, and maintain a high quality of life despite health challenges.

Pain Management: Pain management techniques, including cognitive-behavioural interventions and relaxation methods, can help individuals manage chronic pain and improve their overall well-being.

The Role of Social Factors

Health psychology recognizes the impact of social factors on health:

Social Support: Social support, whether from friends, family, or a support group, can enhance well-being and help individuals cope with health challenges.

Socioeconomic Status: Socioeconomic factors, such as income and education, play a significant role in health disparities. Health psychologists study these disparities and work to address them.

Cultural Considerations: Cultural factors can influence health behaviours and beliefs about illness. Health psychology takes cultural diversity into account when designing interventions.

Challenges and Ethical Considerations

Health psychology faces challenges, including the ethical dilemma of balancing autonomy with the well-being of patients, addressing health disparities, and navigating the growing influence of technology in health care. Ethical considerations are fundamental to maintaining trust and ensuring that the best interests of patients are upheld.

The Future of Health Psychology

The future of health psychology involves addressing the mental health challenges associated with the changing landscape of healthcare and technology, as well as promoting preventive approaches to health and wellness.

Health psychology plays a crucial role in understanding the mind-body connection and promoting wellness and well-being. Understanding the principles of health psychology can empower individuals to make healthier choices, manage stress, and cope with health challenges, contributing to a higher quality of life.

Chapter 16: Environmental Psychology: Exploring the Human-Nature Connection

Environmental psychology is a field that investigates how the physical environment, including natural and built spaces, influences human behaviour, well-being, and overall quality of life. In this chapter, we explore the principles of environmental psychology and its role in understanding the intricate relationship between people and their surroundings.

The Influence of the Environment

Environmental psychology recognizes the significant impact of the environment on human experience and behaviour. Key concepts in this field include:

Place Attachment: Place attachment refers to the emotional bonds people form with specific places. It can influence behaviour, decisions, and well-being.

Environmental Perception and Cognition: Environmental psychologist's studies how people perceive, interpret, and navigate their physical surroundings. Understanding these processes can enhance the design of spaces.

Restorative Environments: Certain natural environments, such as parks and natural landscapes, can have a restorative effect on people, reducing stress and enhancing cognitive functioning.

Environmental Stressors: On the other hand, environmental stressors like noise, pollution, and overcrowding can lead to adverse psychological and physical outcomes.

The Role of Built Environments

Environmental psychology extends to the design and planning of built environments, including homes, workplaces, and urban spaces:

Residential Environments: This area focuses on how the design and layout of homes influence comfort, well-being, and social interactions.

Work Environments: Understanding the impact of workplace design on employee productivity, satisfaction, and well-being is a central concern.

Urban Planning: Urban and environmental psychologists collaborate with urban planners to create cities and communities that promote physical activity, social interaction, and well-being.

Sustainable Design: Sustainable design principles seek to create environments that minimize harm to the natural world, promote energy efficiency, and encourage eco-friendly behaviours.

Environmental Behaviour and Conservation

Environmental psychology explores the motivations and barriers related to pro-environmental behaviours, such as recycling, energy conservation, and sustainable transportation. It also addresses the promotion of conservation efforts and the protection of natural environments.

The Role of Nature in Mental Health

The therapeutic benefits of nature, often referred to as "Eco therapy" or "green therapy," are a significant focus of environmental psychology. Spending time in natural environments can reduce stress, anxiety, and symptoms of depression while enhancing overall well-being.

Challenges and Ethical Considerations

Environmental psychology faces challenges related to the ethical treatment of the environment, ensuring access to green spaces, and addressing environmental injustices. Ethical considerations involve recognizing the rights of nature and promoting equitable access to nature's benefits.

The Future of Environmental Psychology

The future of environmental psychology includes addressing the psychological impact of urbanization, climate change, and technological advances on the human-environment relationship. It also involves advancing sustainable design and promoting pro-environmental behaviours.

Environmental psychology plays a pivotal role in enhancing our understanding of how the environment influences human behaviour, well-being, and quality of life. It provides valuable insights into designing spaces that promote health and happiness while encouraging sustainable practices that protect the natural world.

Chapter 17: Cross-Cultural Psychology: Understanding Human Diversity

Cross-cultural psychology is a field that examines the influence of culture on human behaviour, cognition, and development. It explores the diverse ways in which culture shapes our thoughts, emotions, and actions and the impact of cultural diversity on our globalized world. In this chapter, we delve into the principles of cross-cultural psychology and its role in fostering understanding and respect among different cultures.

Culture and Human Behaviour

Culture is a complex and multifaceted concept that encompasses shared beliefs, values, practices, customs, and ways of life. Key aspects of culture in cross-cultural psychology include:

Cultural Norms and Values: Cultural norms are shared rules and expectations that guide behaviour, while cultural values are the principles that cultures hold dear.

Cultural Identity: Cultural identity is the sense of belonging to a particular culture or group and is an essential component of an individual's self-concept.

Cultural Diversity: Cultural diversity highlights the wide array of cultures and subcultures across the world, each with its unique customs, languages, and traditions.

Cross-Cultural Research Methods

Cross-cultural psychologists use various research methods to understand cultural influences:

Comparative Studies: Comparative studies compare cultural groups to identify similarities and differences in behaviour and cognition.

Cultural Dimensions: Cultural dimensions, such as individualism-collectivism, power distance, and uncertainty avoidance, provide frameworks for understanding cultural variations.

Ethnographic Research: Ethnographic research involves immersing researchers in a specific culture to gain an in-depth understanding of its customs and way of life.

Cross-Cultural Surveys: Cross-cultural surveys collect data from participants across different cultures to examine variations in attitudes, beliefs, and behaviours.

Cultural Neuroscience: Cultural neuroscience investigates how cultural experiences shape neural processes and brain structure.

Culture and Psychology

Culture influences various psychological domains:

Cognition: Culture impacts cognitive processes, such as perception, memory, and problem-solving. It can shape the way people perceive and understand the world.

Emotion: Cultural norms and values influence emotional expression and regulation. Cultural differences can be seen in how emotions are expressed and interpreted.

Social Behaviour: Social behaviour, including interpersonal relationships, communication styles, and social norms, varies across cultures.

Development: Culture plays a significant role in child-rearing practices, socialization, and the development of self-concept.

Understanding Stereotypes and Prejudice

Cross-cultural psychology addresses stereotypes, prejudice, and discrimination by examining their cultural roots and impact. It seeks to promote tolerance and cultural understanding to reduce biases and promote inclusivity.

Challenges and Ethical Considerations

Cross-cultural psychology faces challenges related to ethnocentrism, cultural biases in research, and the need for culturally sensitive practices in the field. Ethical considerations include ensuring that research is respectful and not exploitative of cultural groups.

The Future of Cross-Cultural Psychology

The future of cross-cultural psychology involves exploring the impact of globalization, migration, and technological advancements on cultural interactions and identity. It also focuses on fostering cultural competence and facilitating respectful interactions among diverse cultural groups.

Cross-cultural psychology is an essential field for promoting cultural understanding, tolerance, and respect in our globalized world. It offers valuable insights into the profound impact of culture on human behaviour and provides tools for bridging cultural divides and promoting harmonious interactions among diverse cultural groups.

Chapter 18: Social Psychology:
Exploring the Power of Social Influence

Social psychology is a field that delves into the study of how social interactions, group dynamics, and the presence of others affect our thoughts, feelings, and behaviours. It explores the complex web of human social relationships and the various ways in which we are influenced by the social world around us. In this chapter, we delve into the principles of social psychology and its role in understanding human behaviour in a social context.

The Power of Social Influence

Social psychology recognizes the power of social influence and interaction. Key concepts in this field include:

Conformity: Conformity is the tendency to change one's behaviour, beliefs, or attitudes to match those of others in a group. It explores why people often go along with the crowd.

Obedience: Obedience involves following the orders or commands of an authority figure. It was famously studied by Stanley Milgram, revealing the extent to which people may obey authority, even when it conflicts with their moral values.

Social Norms: Social norms are unwritten rules and expectations governing behaviour within a group or society. They shape our actions and decisions.

Social Roles: Social roles are the positions individuals occupy in a group or society. They come with expectations that influence behaviour.

Group Dynamics: Group dynamics examines how individuals behave in groups, including issues like leadership, communication, decision-making, and conflict resolution.

Attitudes and Attitude Change

Social psychology explores attitudes, their formation, and how they can be changed. Key aspects include:

Attitude Formation: Attitudes are formed through a combination of cognitive, affective, and behavioural components. They can be influenced by socialization and experience.

Persuasion: Persuasion involves changing attitudes through communication and influence techniques. Understanding the factors that make persuasion effective is a central focus of social psychology.

Prejudice and Discrimination: Social psychology addresses the origins and consequences of prejudice, stereotypes, and discrimination. It explores how these biases can be reduced.

Interpersonal Attraction: Interpersonal attraction examines the factors that draw people to one another, such as physical attractiveness, similarity, and proximity.

Group Behaviour and Cooperation

Social psychology explores how groups influence behaviour and decision-making:

Groupthink: Groupthink is a phenomenon where group members prioritize consensus and harmony over critical evaluation, leading to flawed decision-making.

Social Identity: Social identity theory explains how individuals categorize themselves and others into social groups, influencing their behaviour and attitudes.

Cooperation and Conflict: Social psychology examines the dynamics of cooperation, competition, and conflict resolution in social interactions.

Challenges and Ethical Considerations

Social psychology faces challenges related to ethical conduct in research, addressing issues of deception and harm. Ethical considerations include ensuring the welfare and informed consent of research participants.

The Future of Social Psychology

The future of social psychology involves exploring the impact of technology, social media, and globalization on social interactions and influence. It also focuses on applying social psychology principles to address societal issues like prejudice, inequality, and intergroup conflicts.

Social psychology offers insights into the complex web of human social interactions, the power of social influence, and the ways in which we are shaped by our social environments. Understanding its principles can empower individuals to navigate the social world more effectively, fostering harmonious relationships and informed decision-making.

Chapter 19: Personality Psychology: Unravelling the Mysteries of Individual Differences

Personality psychology is a field that investigates the enduring patterns of thoughts, emotions, and behaviours that make each person unique. It explores the factors that shape personality, the various approaches to personality theory, and the significance of understanding individual differences. In this chapter, we delve into the principles of personality psychology and its role in unravelling the mysteries of human uniqueness.

Understanding Personality

Personality encompasses a wide array of traits, characteristics, and patterns of behaviour. Key concepts in personality psychology include:

Trait Theory: Trait theory posits that personality consists of a set of stable traits or dimensions, such as extraversion, neuroticism, and conscientiousness, which define individual differences.

Personality Development: Personality psychologists study the development of personality across the lifespan, from infancy to old age.

Nature vs. Nurture: The debate of nature versus nurture explores the extent to which genetic factors and environmental influences shape personality.

Self-Concept: Self-concept is an individual's perception of themselves, encompassing self-esteem and self-efficacy.

Defence Mechanisms: Defence mechanisms are psychological strategies used to protect the self from distressing thoughts or emotions, such as denial and projection.

Approaches to Personality

Personality psychology encompasses various approaches to understanding personality:

Psychodynamic Theories: Psychodynamic theories, pioneered by Sigmund Freud, explore the unconscious mind, conflict, and the influence of early experiences on personality.

Humanistic Theories: Humanistic theories, including those of Carl Rogers and Abraham Maslow, emphasize self-actualization, personal growth, and the inherent goodness of individuals.

Behavioural and Social-Cognitive Theories: Behavioural and social-cognitive theories examine how behaviours are learned and shaped through environmental factors and social learning.

Trait Theories: Trait theories categorize personality into dimensions or traits, aiming to measure and describe individual differences.

Biological and Evolutionary Theories: Biological and evolutionary theories explore the influence of genetic, neurological, and evolutionary factors on personality.

Personality Assessment

Personality psychology includes various methods for assessing personality, such as self-report questionnaires, interviews, and projective tests. The goal is to measure and analyse personality traits and characteristics.

Applications of Personality Psychology

Personality psychology has practical applications in areas like clinical psychology, counselling, organizational psychology, and educational psychology. It informs therapeutic approaches, career assessments, and personal development.

Challenges and Ethical Considerations

Personality psychology faces challenges related to cultural and gender biases in personality assessments, ethical considerations in clinical practice, and privacy concerns in personality testing. Ethical practice is essential for preserving the integrity of personality psychology.

The Future of Personality Psychology

The future of personality psychology involves integrating modern neuroscience, genetics, and technology to gain a deeper understanding of personality. It also includes addressing the dynamic nature of personality and its adaptation to life's changing circumstances.

Personality psychology sheds light on the enduring patterns that define each individual and offers insights into personal development, self-awareness, and the complexities of human nature. Understanding its principles can help individuals embrace their uniqueness and appreciate the diversity of personalities in the world.

The End